To my mother, Barbara

Text and illustrations copyright © Emma Damon 2019

First published in Great Britain and in the USA in 2019 by
Otter-Barry Books, Little Orchard, Burley Gate, Herefordshire, HR1 3QS
www.otterbarrybooks.com

A catalogue record for this book is available from the British Library.

ISBN 978-1-91095-917-6

Illustrated with watercolour

Set in ArcherPro

Printed in China

1 3 5 7 9 8 6 4 2

THE WONDERFUL WORLD OF CLOTHES

EMMA DAMON

Contents

Otter-Barry BOOKS

Why Do We Wear Clothes?

We wear clothes to keep warm – or cool – or to stay dry, and sometimes to avoid sunburn. Clothes can show what part of the world you live in, which community you are part of or even what sort of person you are.

You can learn a lot about people from their clothes.

Clothes can show if you're going to school, or to a party. You can wear clothes to make you look like everyone else or to look different.

So let's explore the wonderful world of clothes!

When It's Hot

When it's very hot, clothes can help us keep cool and protect us from the sun.

This Italian family need hats, cotton shirts and sun-cream for their summer picnic.

The Maasai people of East Africa wear loose clothes to keep the sun and dust away. Their bright colours are red for energy, blue for the sky and green for the land.

The Tuareg people, who live in the Sahara Desert, wear flowing robes that help to keep layers of cool air between their bodies and the hot sun. Men partly cover their faces against the heat and dust.

This Mexican mother carries her baby in a wrap called a *rebozo*. She ties it over one shoulder and under the other. Made of thin, strong cloth, it keeps the baby cool. Her friend uses her rebozo to carry a kilo of oranges!

What do you like wearing when it's hot?

When It's Cold

In cold weather it is important to keep our bodies warm.
Our thin skins don't protect us from cold air and icy winds.
We need to cover up!

These Swiss children keep warm with down-filled jackets, hats with ear-flaps, gloves and fur-lined boots.

Children in Siberia go out to play wearing padded coats made of wool and embroidered with bright patterns.

Long woollen coats called *chuba* keep people warm in the high mountains of Tibet. They are tied with a sash and often have colourful patterns.

In winter the Inuit of Greenland and Canada wear several layers of clothing made of fur and leather from animals, including caribou and seals.

What do you wear when you go out to play in the winter?

Off To School

School uniforms show which school you go to and can help you feel you belong. Most schools choose a special colour for their uniforms, though some don't have a uniform at all.

In this British school the children wear sweatshirts showing the school logo.

The children in this school in the USA choose what they wear – but the school does have a dress code. You can't turn up in a clown suit!

For art classes, these children in Kolkata, India, wear smocks over their uniforms.

In Australia hats are part of the uniform.

Russian children choose their own style of hat, often a *ushanka*, which has flaps to keep their ears warm.

School children in the United Arab Emirates, as in many other countries, wear uniforms with blazers.

Primary school children in Barbados wear lightweight uniforms: tunics and blouses, shorts and shirts.

What do you wear to school?

Sports and Games

Anyone for cricket, football, netball, beach volleyball? There are hundreds of different outfits made for sports and games. They help you to do your best – and keep you comfortable when you're moving fast.

VOLLEYBALL
For this game you'll need to wear light breathable fabric, so it doesn't cling to you when you're hot.

SWIMMING
Swimsuits are often made of Lycra, a fabric which stretches and fits the body well in water. Swimming goggles help protect your eyes from chlorine in the swimming pool.

FOOTBALL
Footballers wear shirts, shorts and socks in the colours of their team and with its logo. Lots of fans buy the same outfit to show their support, with their favourite player's squad number on the back.

ICE-SKATING

Performers on ice often wear brightly coloured skating costumes as part of their show. Lace-up leather boots with jagged teeth blades, called toe picks, complete their outfit.

CRICKET

In the past, cricketers played in all-white clothing, except for a team cap and badge. Nowadays players often wear outfits in different team colours, even for important matches.

SKIING

When skiing, it's a good idea to wear a padded waterproof suit and gloves, along with a pair of goggles and a helmet. Choose bright colours, so people can see you coming in the snow!

What do you wear for your favourite sport?

Special Jobs

Many jobs need protective clothing. Special outfits make it possible for people to work even in dangerous or extreme places – like outer space.

POLAR EXPLORER

To work in the Arctic or Antarctic you need several layers of light but wind-and-waterproof fabric, both natural and man-made, to keep your body warm from head to toes and let you move freely. Goggles protect your eyes from bright sunlight.

FIREFIGHTER

Firefighters must wear tough, fireproof and waterproof clothes that are easy to move about in. Their garments are made of three-layered fireproof material, usually bright yellow, to be easily seen in the dark.

ASTRONAUT
Spacesuits like this NASA Mark 111 model give total protection so that astronauts can breathe and survive extremes of heat and cold when outside the spacecraft. Inside the suit they wear a special cooling and ventilation garment. Air and water are supplied from the backpack.

UNDERWATER PHOTOGRAPHER
This photographer is scuba-diving, to film a coral reef. Her wetsuit is made of foam-lined neoprene that keeps her warm and helps protect against jellyfish stings. Her flippers give her super-long feet to propel her along.

Can you think of other jobs that need special clothing?

Six Great Religions

There are many faiths and religions, in addition to the six described here. Some people wear clothes that show which religion they belong to.

Hindu men in South Asia and elsewhere often wear a skirt-like garment called a *dhoti*, and women wear colourful *saris*. Even when they wear western-style clothes, Hindus may draw a red dot, called a *tilak* or, for women only, a *bindi* on their forehead.

Most Christians don't wear special clothing. They wear smart clothes to go to church. Priests and ministers, both men and women, sometimes wear special white collars known as 'dog-collars', and they wear long robes when they take a service (see page 20).

The *daastar* or turban is worn by all Sikh men and sometimes nowadays by women too. It can be seven metres long when unrolled!

In the Jewish faith, most people dress in western-style clothes, though men and boys wear a small round cap called a *kippah* when they go to the synagogue. Some Jewish groups wear plain black clothes.

Many Muslim women wear the *burqa*, a black robe covering the body and head, and sometimes with only a narrow opening for the eyes. Muslim schoolgirls often wear a *hijab*, a long scarf covering their hair and shoulders, to match their uniforms.

Buddhist monks wear a robe of orange cloth. The orange or saffron colour was chosen long ago because a dye of this colour could be easily made from saffron crocus flowers.

Is there a religious event where you might wear special clothes?

Special Occasions

Special events need special clothes. Sometimes it has to be a particular garment, like a christening robe. Other times, you just wear your smartest clothes.

At a Buddhist naming ceremony, a baby is brought to the temple to have his or her name announced to relatives and friends. Coloured threads are sometimes tied round the baby's wrists to show he or she is protected by a good spirit.

In a Christian baptism or christening service, the baby will wear a white gown and shawl, often handed down through families. If an older child or a grown-up is baptised, they may wear white, or just a smart outfit.

Jewish children celebrate *bar-mitzvah* (for boys) and *bat-mitzvah* (for girls) around the age of twelve. With their best clothes the boys wear a *kippah* and girls sometimes wear a lace head-covering. Both wear tasselled shawls, called *tallit*.

At a traditional Muslim wedding the bride wears a *hijab* or head-covering to show modesty. The groom wears *salwar kameez*, a highly decorated tunic worn with loose trousers.

At this Chinese wedding the bride and groom both wear red robes. Red is seen as a lucky colour.

At a Sikh wedding, the bride wears a gold embroidered *chuni* (shawl) to cover her head. The groom will wear a red or dark pink turban and carries a scarf called a *pulla,* which the bride will also hold, as a sign of union.

Have you ever been to a wedding? What did you wear?

Dressing Up For Festivals

Festivals are days of celebration, with parades and feasts – and often special costumes as well.

Many countries celebrate Hallowe'en on 31st October. Children dress up as witches or ghosts and go from house to house after dark, trick-or-treating, and they're often given sweets or other treats.

In **SWEDEN**, on St Lucia's Day, 13th December, a girl is chosen to represent St Lucia, who brings light to the world at its darkest time. She will wear a long white dress with a red sash, and a crown fitted with up to nine lighted candles.

TET TRUNG THU, the Vietnamese Moon Festival, is celebrated on a night of full moon in mid-autumn. Children dress up in their best clothes or fancy dress. They parade with colourful moon masks, lanterns and balloons, and eat Moon Cakes! It's a big event in China too.

MEXICO'S Day of the Dead is held between October 31st and November 2nd, with parades and celebrations as people honour those who have passed away. Popular costumes feature skulls and bones – or girls may have painted faces, with ribbons and flowers in their hair.

CHINESE New Year is based on the appearance of the new moon between 21st January and 20th February, and lasts for 15 days. Sometimes as many as 100 people join to make a dragon that parades through the streets. A traditional dragon costume is made of embroidered silk. Everyone dresses up in new clothes and red is the favourite colour, for joy and good fortune in the year ahead.

Do you have a favourite festival that you celebrate at school?

From Head to Toe

Hats and head-coverings can tell us a lot about the person underneath. And shoes can do more than keep your feet dry!

NIQAB - A veil worn by many Muslim women, that may almost cover the face.

COWBOY OR STETSON HAT – Made of felt, with a big brim and worn in western USA.

CHEF'S HAT – Known as a 'toque'. In a big restaurant kitchen, the top chef has the tallest hat.

CHULLO OR ANDEAN HAT – Made in Peru from Alpaca wool.

ROYAL CROWN – The British Queen's crown is made of gold, with 2,868 diamonds, 273 pearls and 17 sapphires.

BASEBALL CAP – The long brim shields the player's eyes from the sun. But some people like to wear it back to front!

PERUVIAN BOWLER HAT – These English-style hats are worn by many women in Peru and Bolivia.

KOFIA HAT – A flat-topped hat worn by men in East Africa, made of embroidered wool or fabric.

WOOLLY CAT HAT – Fun, hand-knitted children's hat. Would you like to wear this?

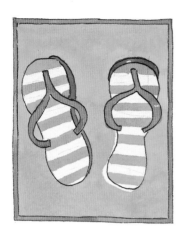

FLIP-FLOPS – Rubber sandals with a toe-strap. Leather flip-flops were worn in Ancient Egypt.

WELLINGTON BOOTS – These waterproof rubber boots are named after a British duke – but his were black leather.

SANDALS – These are the oldest kind of shoe, dating from around 10,000 years ago.

HIGH-HEELED SHOES – These are smart shoes for women. The heels can be up to 25cm (10 inches) high.

TIGER SLIPPERS – Traditional slippers, still often worn by Chinese children. The tigers are to scare away anything nasty.

BROGUES – Leather lace-up shoes with low heels and a pattern of dots in the leather.

COWBOY BOOTS – Riding boots from western USA, made from leather which has been decorated with a pattern.

SNEAKERS OR TRAINERS – Made of rubber and artificial fabrics. Originally for sports, they are now often a fashion item, worn all over the world.

BALLET SHOES – Very lightweight shoes for female dancers, with hard points so they can stand on their toes.

Jewellery and Decorations

Jewellery can be anything that decorates or adorns our bodies, and it's worn by both men and women – from rings and bracelets to hair-clips and body piercings.

KARA – A steel bracelet worn by Sikh men, usually on the right arm.

HAIR CLIPS - made of coloured clay or plastic, these add to the hairstyles of women and men of the Bana tribe in Ethiopia.

OPAL PENDANT – Opals are multi-coloured silica stones, sacred to the Aboriginal people of Australia, and made into all kinds of jewellery, like this pendant.

HAMSA – A hand-shaped symbol worn mainly in the Middle East and parts of Africa, to give good luck.

MEHNDI – A kind of paste with which a design can be made on the skin, and washed off again. It is very popular in India and Pakistan, for both men and women.

NECK RINGS – These rings of gold or brass are traditionally worn by girls and women of the Padaung tribe in Thailand and Myanmar.

TIKI PENDANT – Made from jade or greenstone by the Maori people in New Zealand, this pendant represents the first man on Earth.

GOLD EARRINGS – These very large earrings are worn by the Fulani women of West Africa.

BLACK PEARLS – This black pearl necklace is from Tahiti, using pearls from the black-lip oyster.

AMBER NECKLACE – This necklace is from Tibet. Amber is fossilised tree resin, and to Tibetans it is a sign of energy and power.

SILVER NECKLACE – From Taxco, a silver-mining town in Mexico, these necklaces are crafted by modern designers, based on ancient Mayan designs.

SOLAH SHRINGAR – sixteen adornment rituals for beautifying Hindu brides, including bracelets, necklaces, nose-rings and earrings.

TURQUOISE EARRINGS – These earrings are from the Navajo people in north America. In Navajo legend the turquoise is called 'the fallen sky stone'.

FRIENDSHIP BRACELETS – These are made from cotton and beads and are exchanged as a sign of friendship by children all over the world. Have you ever given one to your friends?

Buttons, Belts and Wraps

There are so many ways to fasten and unfasten clothing. Buttons have been used for thousands of years, while zips are a much more recent invention.

CHINESE FROG BUTTON – A loop of fabric goes round the button.

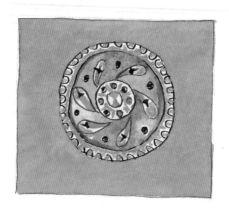

CLOISONNÉ BUTTON – A metal button with a painted enamel surface.

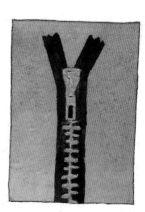

ZIP FASTENER – Invented in the USA in the 19th century and perfected in the 20th century. Billions are made every year for all kinds of clothes.

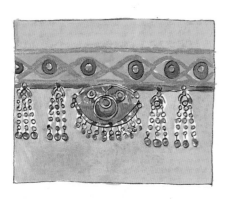

KUCHI BELTS – These are decorative ornamental belts originally made in Afghanistan, using pieces of mirror glass, shiny coins or metal shapes, and rich embroidery.

PRESS STUDS OR SNAP FASTENERS – These are often used instead of buttons nowadays, especially on young children's and casual clothing.

ADINKRA – This is a Ghanaian craft, using many symbols like this duafe, or comb, painted on a fabric-covered button.

MOROCCAN BUTTONS – Made from knotted silk, these are used to decorate traditional garments, like the kaftan.

FIBULA BROOCH – Often made with Celtic designs, this brooch is rather like a big safety pin. Used to fasten a scarf or shawl, it has a long history, going back to the Ancient Greeks.

SATSUMA BUTTONS – These are made in Japan from baked clay, then glazed and painted.

A KIMONO

The kimono is a traditional Japanese robe, worn by men as well as women. When you tie a kimono, it is important to do it according to the rules. The belt worn with it is called an *obi*.

HOW TO WEAR A KIMONO

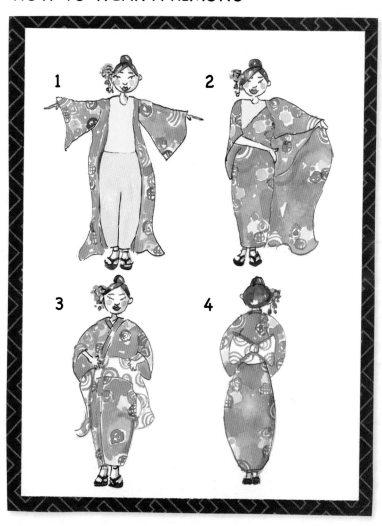

HOW TO WEAR A SARI

SARI

A sari is a dress made from a single piece of material, without stitching. It can use up to eight metres of fabric. Its origins have been traced back over four thousand years to the Indus Valley, stretching from present-day Afghanistan through Pakistan to India. Saris are now worn by women round the world. Unlike the kimono, they can be folded in many different ways.

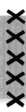

Fabulous Fabrics

We use hundreds of different fabrics in our clothes, but there are two main types: natural fabrics made from plants and animal hair, and man-made fabrics made in factories or hand-made from raw materials.

WOOL comes from the fleece of a sheep, collected, cleaned and spun into cloth. This Scottish shepherd is keeping warm with a sheep's wool hat, gloves and scarf.

Cashmere is a very soft kind of wool made from the hair of Cashmere goats in Himalayan and Asian countries.

Alpaca wool, from the fleece of Alpacas in South America, is a thick kind of wool. This farmer in Peru is wearing an Alpaca poncho. The brown and grey colours are created from a dye using plants and minerals.

COTTON is harvested from the cotton plant, grown in America and Australia and some other countries. After it is picked, it is spun into fabric and made into all kinds of clothes, including shirts, T-shirts, jumpers, trousers, dresses and underwear. It is very comfortable to wear as it allows the skin to breathe. It is one of the most widely-used fabrics for clothes throughout the world.

SILK – Mulberry leaves are picked to feed silkworms. From their cocoons come the fine threads of this beautiful, soft and long-lasting fabric. First made in China five thousand years ago, silk was so precious that the way to make it was kept secret for many centuries.

MAN-MADE OR SYNTHETIC FABRICS are also widely used in making clothes, sometimes mixed with natural fabrics. The best-known types are nylon, rayon, polyester, Lurex and Lycra. These fabrics are made in factories and are often shinier, more stretchy or tougher than natural fabrics. Fabrics such as Lycra are excellent for sportswear, being light, hard-wearing and supporting the body during exercise.

What kind of fabrics do you like wearing best?

The Life of a Pair of Jeans

Jeans get their name from the Italian city of Genoa, where a kind of cloth called 'jean' was made from cotton. They were first made in the USA in 1871 as tough work trousers to be worn by gold-miners.

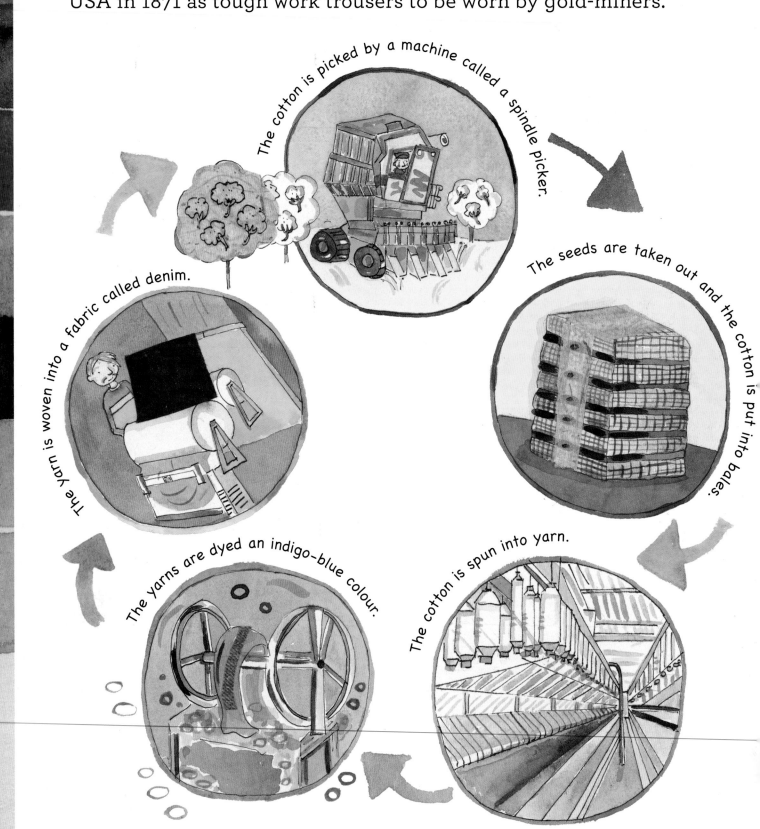

The cotton is picked by a machine called a spindle picker.

The seeds are taken out and the cotton is put into bales.

The cotton is spun into yarn.

The yarns are dyed an indigo-blue colour.

The yarn is woven into a fabric called denim.

Then the denim fabric is cut and sewn into a pair of jeans.

They are delivered to stores all over the world.

An average pair of jeans takes only 15 minutes to make in a factory, using 15 pieces of individual cloth.

What activities do you do when you're wearing jeans?

Recycling Clothes

A lot of our clothes, such as cotton and wool, come from 'sustainable' sources, like plants and animals. But with over seven billion people in the world, we need to recycle as much as possible. Today's old clothes can be tomorrow's new ones!

In Kenya, Uganda and Ethiopia, sandals are being made from old tyres, and even sold on the internet.

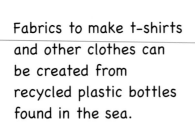

Shiploads of old clothes travel from India to countries where they can be recycled into new fabrics and made into new clothes.

Fabrics to make t-shirts and other clothes can be created from recycled plastic bottles found in the sea.

Here is a second-hand clothes market in Paris. People enjoy finding 'vintage' clothes, from their parents' or grandparents' time, to give the clothes a new lease of life.

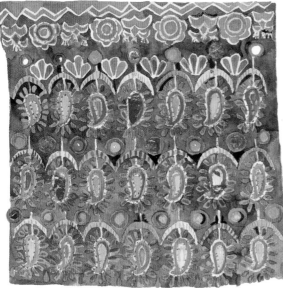

In Pakistan, old saris and beaded fabrics are recycled into beautiful bags.

This girl is making an old denim jacket 'new' by adding other fabrics to it. This is called upcycling.

Why not try out ideas for recycling clothes with beads or decorations, with your family?

Technology and the Future

21st century technology is amazing. And it is changing the way clothes are made and designed. Fashion designers and scientists are finding ways to make our clothes better than ever, using new technology to create amazing new fabrics and designs.

There's Lycra sportswear that glows in the dark, for night events.

This fashion model is wearing an amazing dress created from a 3d printer.

This girl is wearing modern techno breathable fabric for her Yoga class.

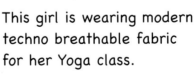

Space-age fabrics, made into gloves and socks, trap body heat to keep us warm.

Whatever happens next, the future for clothes is exciting. Who knows what we'll be wearing in 100 years' time?

Maybe now you'll be inspired to design clothes yourself!

Glossary

Cashmere – A fine, soft wool made from the coat of a Kashmir goat.

Cocoon – A case of spun thread, protecting the pupa stage of an insect's transformation from larva (like silkworm) to moth.

Cotton – A soft white fibre from the cotton plant made into textiles and thread for sewing.

Denim – A hardwearing fabric, usually dyed blue, named for the French city of Nîmes.

Down – Fine soft feathers used to make a warm insulating layer.

Fabric – Woven material of any kind, that can be soft or stiff.

Felt – A kind of cloth made by rolling and pressing wool or synthetic fibres.

Fibre – Either a single thread of cloth, or cloth made up of such threads.

Indigo – A blue dye originally obtained from the indigo plant but nowadays often synthetic.

Lycra – An elastic synthetic fibre or fabric used especially for making close-fitting sports clothing.

Neoprene – A synthetic rubber-like material.

Poncho – A South American cape made from a single piece of cloth, with a head-hole.

Recycling – Taking old or waste materials and reforming them into new products.

Silk – A strong, soft lustrous fibre produced by silkworms, used to make thread and fabric.

Sustainable – Can be naturally replaced, so does not reduce the Earth's resources.

Synthetic – Human-made, by combining chemicals. The opposite of Natural.

Wool – Soft hair from the coat of a sheep or goat used for making cloth and yarn.

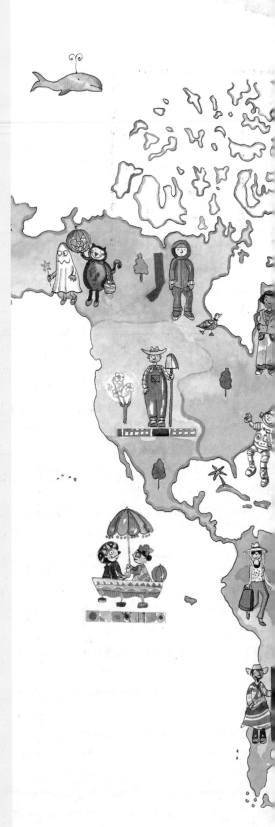